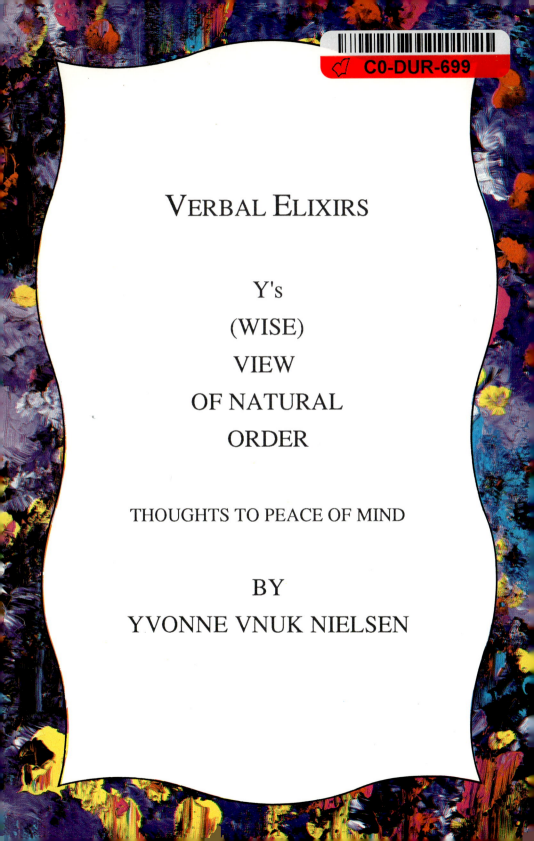

Verbal Elixirs

Y's

(WISE)

VIEW

OF NATURAL

ORDER

THOUGHTS TO PEACE OF MIND

BY

YVONNE VNUK NIELSEN

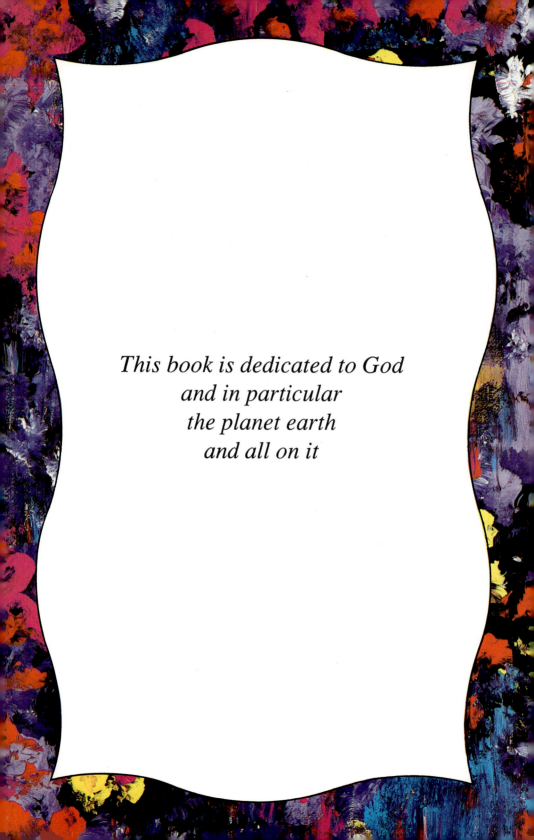

This book is dedicated to God
and in particular
the planet earth
and all on it

Much thanks and
gratitude to the
"Wise Guys"
whose wisdom
gave me
the guidance
to learn more
than meets the human eye.

To Goodie,
Gudrun Dawson,
whose faith
at times
was greater
than mine

To
Tammany,
whose pure Love
is a mother's
true gift

To
Keli Moser
for sharing with love
her time and computer wisdom

And to
Crystal St. Louis
For helping get the book
to you

Love

The book is for Love and with Love
To increase Love on earth

To understand Love is to live Love
It's not an act of love as many think

At times, Love doesn't look or sound good
Love is a feeling

To understand your feelings
You must deal with old emotions

Emotions are ways to show (emote) old responses to
    situations
Feelings are your moment to moment barometer to
    new situations

To differentiate between emotions and feelings
You must learn to deal with them and
Not let them deal with you

First come the thoughts
Then see how they can be an enhancing part of your life
You become your thoughts
After you learn to live them

To just think and act will not do
You must feel

Love is a feeling!!!!!!!!!!!!

Learn to replace old negative *emotions* with
Positive Loving *feelings* to be emoted later

Start with the thoughts
Believe them, Live them
And so shall you be

ABOUT THE BOOK

This book is not to be finished

Part of the human condition
Is to continually re-fine one's self

This is a handbook
For that ongoing refinement

Use it to get past the material
And to connect with the *essence* of it all

Learn to do all with Love
And so be one with the bigger picture

Live for the betterment of all
And your life will be richer
Than humanly imaginable

This book is not necessarily
To be read from front to back

Open it anywhere
The higher Principal
Will direct you to the right page

This is not a Fast Read...

If you buzz thru this
You will miss the best part
The Experience

If you can't get into
These verbal elixirs
    You need to be
    less distracted...

To be more focused
Do the following
breathing technique:

Take 3 deep breaths
   (from your gut)
Like a bi-i-i-i-g sigh of relief

Your body does it naturally
Why not get the benefit at will?
Inhale pure white lite (see it feel it)
To see white light
(White molecular energy)
Visualize the snow on a non-working T.V.
   channel
Then add the quality of freshly fallen snow
      when the sun glistens it with colors
It comes in thru the top of your head
And fills up your whole body

As you exhale you will see a black cloud
      of tension leave thru your mouth
Each exhale gets greyer
And the last exhale will be white
Each time you inhale there will be
      more and more white lite in you
With the last inhale the white lite
will be so compact that it will seep
thru your pores and envelope you
as well as blend you with the air
space around you

Be one with the air space around you

            With that sensation
            Go back to experiencing
               the elixirs!

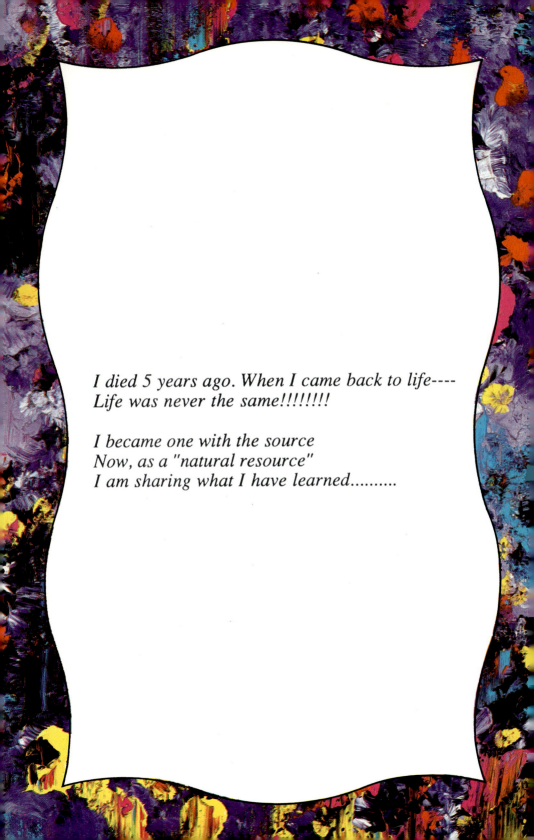

I died 5 years ago. When I came back to life----
Life was never the same!!!!!!!!

I became one with the source
Now, as a "natural resource"
I am sharing what I have learned..........

There is no real order in the cosmos
There is an order of disorder
and so the book goes...

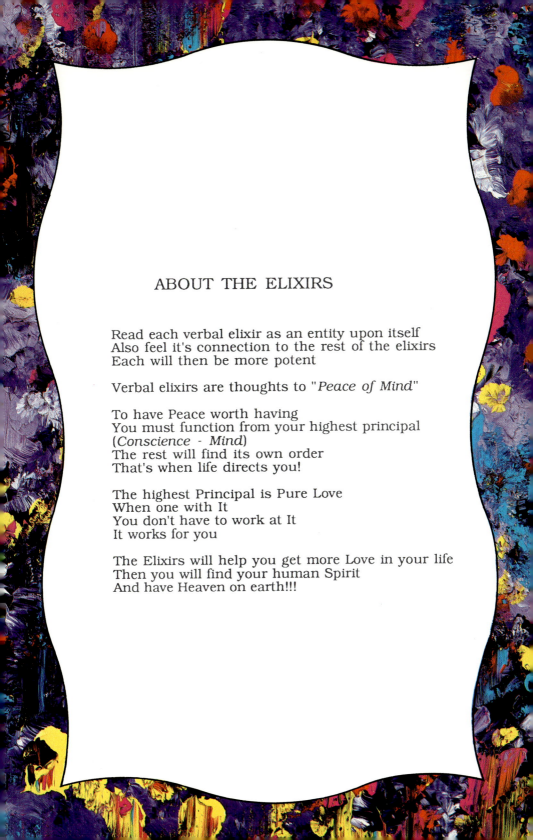

ABOUT THE ELIXIRS

Read each verbal elixir as an entity upon itself
Also feel it's connection to the rest of the elixirs
Each will then be more potent

Verbal elixirs are thoughts to "*Peace of Mind*"

To have Peace worth having
You must function from your highest principal
(*Conscience - Mind*)
The rest will find its own order
That's when life directs you!

The highest Principal is Pure Love
When one with It
You don't have to work at It
It works for you

The Elixirs will help you get more Love in your life
Then you will find your human Spirit
And have Heaven on earth!!!

Each Elixir is a Loving truth
(Love feels good)

Your rhythm and mood effect
How you interpret the elixirs

   So if any elixir doesn't feel good
   It's you
   Not the elixir

Any elixir that causes discomfort
Signifies an area
Where there is room for added in-sight

With each new in-sight
Your world is lighter
You will be more connected
With the bigger picture

See how each elixir can make sense and be a truth
It will help you get beyond programmed thinking
And help you to be even more Loving

The elixirs are basic Truths

For a verbal elixir to work
You must internalize it

To internalize it
You must experience it
Then it can become part of you

The ones that feel right, internalize
See how you can apply it to your day
Then you will be one with it

If you feel better
Share it
And the world will be a better place

Use the elixirs that touch a good spot
At different times
Different elixirs will work
It's up to you to find the right ones

Read with negativity in your heart
And the elixirs will cause discomfort

Read with Love in your heart
And you will find new ways to be even more loving

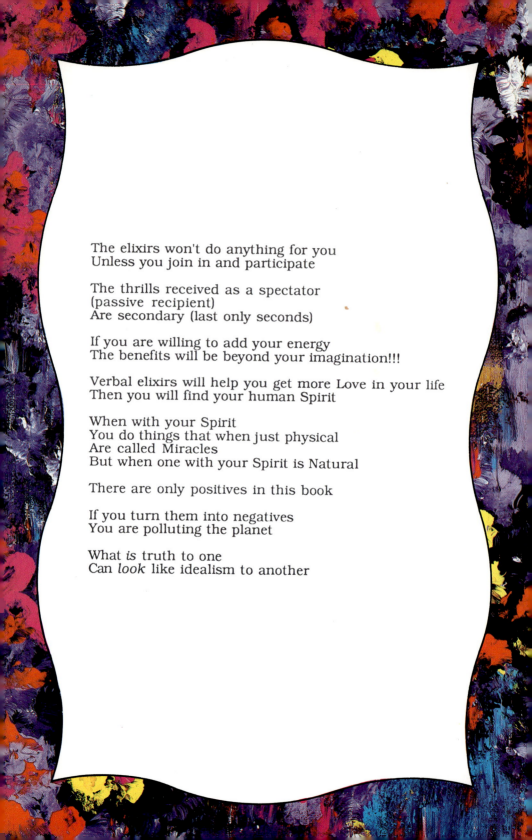

The elixirs won't do anything for you
Unless you join in and participate

The thrills received as a spectator
(passive recipient)
Are secondary (last only seconds)

If you are willing to add your energy
The benefits will be beyond your imagination!!!

Verbal elixirs will help you get more Love in your life
Then you will find your human Spirit

When with your Spirit
You do things that when just physical
Are called Miracles
But when one with your Spirit is Natural

There are only positives in this book

If you turn them into negatives
You are polluting the planet

What *is* truth to one
Can *look* like idealism to another

The elixirs are written
From a Purely Loving
Spiritual Perspective

The physical condition,
In and by itself,
Has many limitations
Some extreme enough
To be *labeled* handicaps

There really is no such thing
As a handicap
Just a chance to creatively find
Wonderful options

From a Spiritual Perspective,
There is only an endless array
     of options

If you can find the truth in the elixirs
And join in the rhythmn of Spritual Love
You too, can have wonderful options
Forever

God doesn't damn anything
God is Love
God *is* The Truth
God's energy is Positive
And the book follows:

Verbal Elixirs

Y'S

(WISE)

VIEW OF NATURAL ORDER

————————————————————————————————

Human race
Don't take it literally
There's no hurry
You have all the time on earth
And more...

It's not so much what you get from your day
But what you bring to it

Don't let others do unto you
What you would not do unto them

To love another
You must first love your self
Otherwise, how can you share what you don't have?

Everyone has learned to use their brain
Some more than others

But how many have learned to use their mind?

Mind is beyond brain

Brain is material
Mind is ethereal

Mind is

To be one with "It all"
You must use your mind
Mind is beyond material

A thought is a thought
An experience is an experience
To be a thought is an experience

How much power does a drop of water taken from the
ocean have?
Alone, it's no more than a drip!!!
Put the drip back in the ocean
Now how much power does it have?
It pays to be one with the bigger picture

To just think
Is like the drip from the ocean
It's missing the power that comes from being
one with "It all"
(Which is a feeling)

When you get to your Mind's eye
You can see forever

Being Spiritual is living religion
Instead of talking and thinking about it

When you get a thought
If it's right
It will be
It's more beyond your control
Than you think

In-sight is where it's at

To be the best you
Learn to listen to your inner self
That got lost "growing to conform"

The material world is only symbolic
Of the rhythm of the inner world

When Spirited
You know there is more than meets the human eye

Don't fake it, ...be it
If it feels right long enough
You're it!!

Life without Love
Leaves one feeling empty
Look at the many ways you try to fill yourself

You may think you have it all
But if you don't have Love *within* you
You really have nothing at all!!!

Thinking is geared to logic
Feeling is geared to Love

Love and logic are sometimes incompatible

To just use your brain
You are no different than a robot
The only options you have are the one's given to you

To Love without self-love
Is a dependency
Maybe even an addiction

No one or nothing can make you feel good
Unless you let it or them

What you think
You are!!!

People of the flesh (material)
Think humans are basically bad

People of the Spirit
Feel humans are basically good

Most pray for something good to happen
And then sit and wait

Pray for something good to happen
Then go and make it happen
And your prayers will be answered!

All are committing suicide
Some slower than others

Life is nothing more than the use
Or misuse of your energy

Misuse brings about dis-ease
Dis-ease long enough is disease

Make the world a better place
Generate the best in you

Radiate or radiation gets you!!!

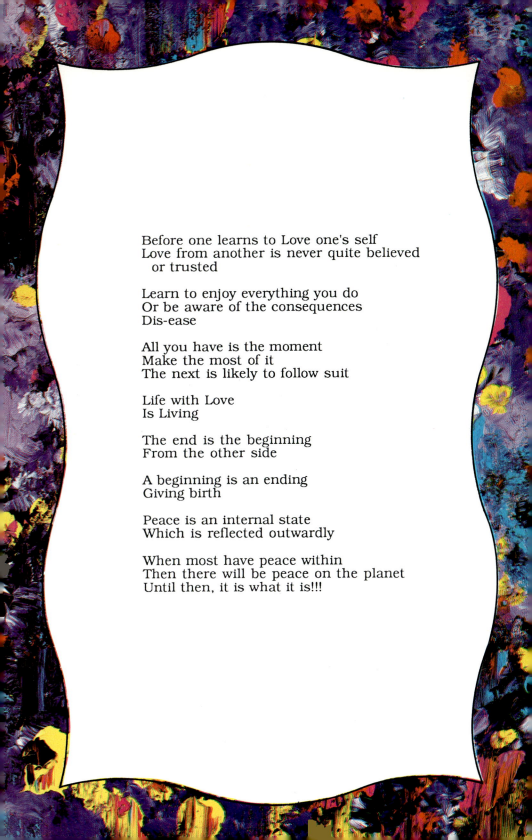

Before one learns to Love one's self
Love from another is never quite believed
  or trusted

Learn to enjoy everything you do
Or be aware of the consequences
Dis-ease

All you have is the moment
Make the most of it
The next is likely to follow suit

Life with Love
Is Living

The end is the beginning
From the other side

A beginning is an ending
Giving birth

Peace is an internal state
Which is reflected outwardly

When most have peace within
Then there will be peace on the planet
Until then, it is what it is!!!

The more sensitive you are
The more aware you are

The more pain you feel
The more Love you feel

Spend minimal time on the pain
Center on the Love

Center on the good
Deal with the negative

Being aware and dealing with negatives
Is how one refines one's self

You are fine
Just keep re-fining

Most fight the flow
While taking from it

Be Lovingly with the flow
And share it instead

People scheme
Rather than finding the scheme
And enhancing it

You may be one out of many
But we are also many out of one

Making the most of the moment
Is all in the attitude

Attitude has a feeling

The rhythm you are in when you die
Is the same rhythm you are in when beyond

Heaven is a rhythm
Not a place

Must have Love
To have spirit

Love is a feeling
Feelings have rhythm

Learn to live The Rhythm

It's not the best things in life are free
It's the best thing in life is being free

Learn to be in control
Of being out of control
By being one with "It all"

As you learn to be the best you
You will also find your way to heaven

Every thing has a frequency
"To be" with Love is your natural vibration

Living pure Love
Is Peace of Mind

With Peace of Mind comes true success

Being one with your spirit is Peace of Mind

Peace of Mind is ecstacy!!!

Center on how you want to be and be it

Learn to reconnect with your Spirit
Love is the way to find it

You must learn to Love your self
Before you can truly Love another
Otherwise how can you share what you don't have?

You must Love your self
To truly believe the Love of another

Talk to your self
Answer too!!!
Otherwise why talk?

Be your own best friend!
Have your self over for dinner!

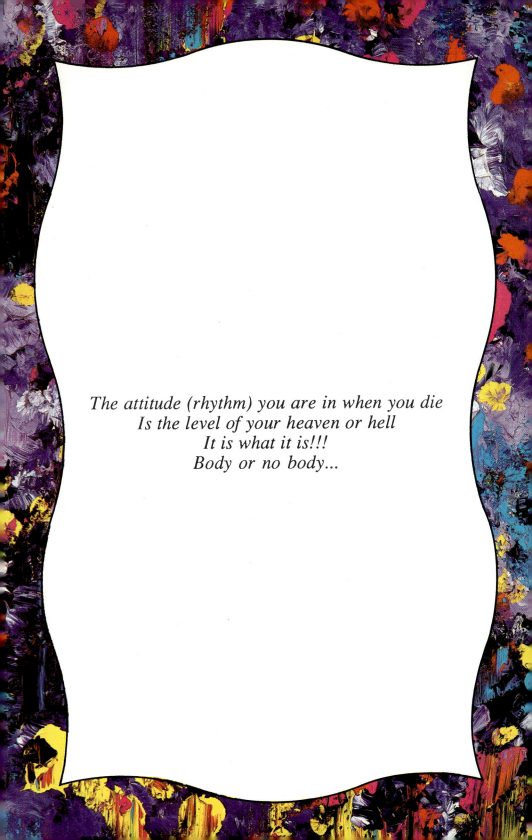

The attitude (rhythm) you are in when you die
Is the level of your heaven or hell
It is what it is!!!
Body or no body...

Everything has positive and negative aspects
Be aware of the negative and deal with them if necessary
Center on and enhance the positives

Ego and spirit are not compatible

Ego is self serving with little or no regard for others

Spirit has your best interest at heart as well as others

You must be your own best friend
You must like your self
You must Love your self

You must have *it* within you to know what *it* is

Talk to your self like a best friend

To change:

   See how you'd like to be
   Get into the details (see your demeanor, other's
   responses, etc.)
   Step into the picture and be it
   Feel, sense the atmosphere,...use all senses
   Whether you do it in your mind or for real
   The results are the same
   The more you rehearse in your mind
   The faster the results

For this technique to truly work
Your goal must be for the enhancement
   of your self and the bigger picture

Love and Wisdom go together
With Love comes Wisdom

Experienced knowledge is wisdom

Life is energy
Spirit gives it focus

There is nothing you can do about anything
Unless you take ultimate responsibility

Greedy is a companion to needy

Only way to satisfaction
Is thru self-Love
The abundance of which is shared

Feelings are a barometer to your self

If you are emotional
You are living that experience in the past

Most are so busy being busy
They lost their purpose

What is your purpose for getting thru each day
Is it just to make it thru the day?

Generate good energy by doing what you do with Love
Others will benefit from the positive vibes

You don't have to Love what you're doing
But do it with Love

If you don't have love in your heart
You must be diplomatic
If you do have love in your heart
You can be honest!

It's Mind over matter
Not brain over matter

Creative is beyond logical

Logic follows and is built on what was
    previously illogical

Best is for the moment
Better is yet to come

Internal human combustion is another force

Spirit and internal human combustion
Are one and the same.

Internal human combustion is reflected in a skip

Get a skip in your life and never lose it

Is the world a better place for your involvement today?
If so, a day well spent
If not, do something with Love

When one has a death experience
The brain isn't working
The Mind is

Most know what to think not how to think

Birds of a feather flock together
Wonder what's wrong with you?
Look at your friends

To have a good day
Share good energy
They're on the same wave length

Do with Love
Not for Love

Your self is your soul

As you learn to be nicer to your soul
You will gain your Spirit

Spirit is pure Love
It comes from the connection
With the bigger picture

Spirit and Mind go hand in hand

Spirit is sharing the abundance of self Love
Which is then other Love

We treat others
The way we treat our self

If you don't Love your self
What you think is Love for another
Is really for love from another

If you are waiting for something good to happen
    in order to feel good
You may have a hell of a long wait!!!

To feel good:
          Remember a time
          When you felt on top of the world
          Or at least good

          Feel it now

Once you've had a feeling (experience)
You can always get it back

When you feel good
Good things are more likely to happen

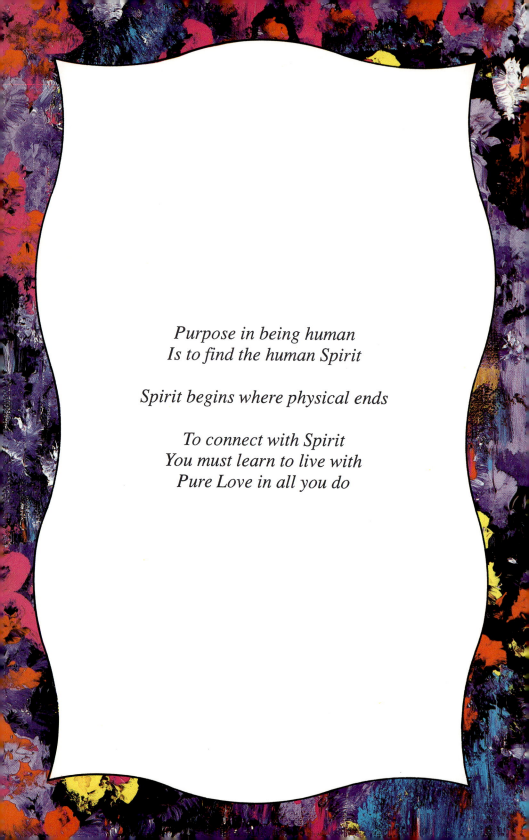

Purpose in being human
Is to find the human Spirit

Spirit begins where physical ends

To connect with Spirit
You must learn to live with
Pure Love in all you do

Everything has a vibration, frequency

Heaven is a rhythm
Not a place

Love has a frequency
God is Love
God and Love are the same frequency

To be one with "It all" (God)
Be Loving in all you do

Love for something is not Pure Love

Pure Love has no expectation

Ego and Spirit are not on the same
    frequency (Wave length)

When one with your Spirit
There is a feeling of effervescence

To understand cosmic law
Is to live it

Feel one with the air space around you
Sense your being blending on a
    molecular level

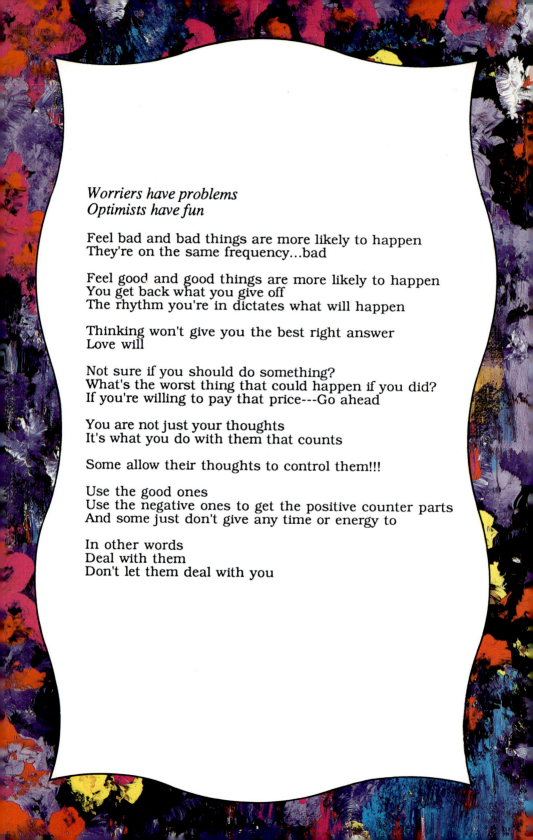

Worriers have problems
Optimists have fun

Feel bad and bad things are more likely to happen
They're on the same frequency...bad

Feel good and good things are more likely to happen
You get back what you give off
The rhythm you're in dictates what will happen

Thinking won't give you the best right answer
Love will

Not sure if you should do something?
What's the worst thing that could happen if you did?
If you're willing to pay that price---Go ahead

You are not just your thoughts
It's what you do with them that counts

Some allow their thoughts to control them!!!

Use the good ones
Use the negative ones to get the positive counter parts
And some just don't give any time or energy to

In other words
Deal with them
Don't let them deal with you

If you think you are just your body
Who do you think gets it up and out each day?

Mind is cosmic
Brain is material
Mind can take you from material to cosmic

It takes Loving faith
Not blind faith

Brain brings pain to awareness
Need to get beyond the pain
Mind is the way

Mind is one with "It all" in the rhythm of Love

If you are one with "It all"
You have the power of "It all"

Mind is Spirit of the brain

Life without Love
Is a slow death

Soul without Spirit is nowhere

Separation is delusion of the human condition

Paradox exists between the 3rd and 4th dimensions

The faster you read this
The less you experience it
The less you get out of it

Maybe faster isn't always better

What you do in one part of your life
Affects all parts of your life

Make the most of what it is
And you will be where you are supposed to be

What one does in particular
Is predicative of what one does in general

If you aren't happy with your self
How can you believe any one else could be

People who are jealous
Usually have no *balls* to go for what they want

You can't work at being creative
Creativity works for you

A playful attitude is not work!!!

Peace of Mind is an ongoing process
Of making the most of the moment

Happiness is all in the attitude
Not in what is happening

Nothing can make you happy
Unless you let it

No one can give you anything
That you don't already have

If you think they can
You are under-estimating your self
You must have it within you to know it

The other side of stubborn
Is committed

Flexibility VS clumsiness

Accident prone?
You are going too fast

Up there and out there
May really be in there

By going further within
You are also farther out

All is one!!!

If you aren't getting the right answers
Ask different questions

You treat others
The way you treat your self

Feeling like a failure?
You will look for faults in others

Words you use create your reality
If you don't like your world
Check your vocabulary

The way we see our self
Colors how we see the rest of the world

Each day do something new
Or do something old in a new way

Limit preconceived ideas
And each day becomes an adventure
Rather than a dreaded habit

Go thru each day with the naiveté of a 6-year old

Too much friction
Diminishes inertia

Aging is due to resistance

Getting to your goals better be enjoyable
Because life is mainly getting there

Reaching a goal
For all rhyme or reason
Is a momentary whoopee!!!
And then on to the next

Learn to enjoy the process!

Happy people take what is
And make the most of the best

If you work hard at something
I bet your not having fun
Or are you a masochist?

When you do negatives
And good things happen
It's luck

When you do good
And good things happen
It's natural order
There's no fear that it may go away
It's consistent with where you are

Less secure within your self
The greater the need to control others

Feel the pain
Become intolerant of it
Then take steps to change
That's a healthy process

Pain brings change

Or you can keep the pain
Numb your feelings
And stay where you are
And that's a slow death

You make choices
On what you want to do
With each situation
Literally, there are endless options

If you feel stuck
You are limiting your options

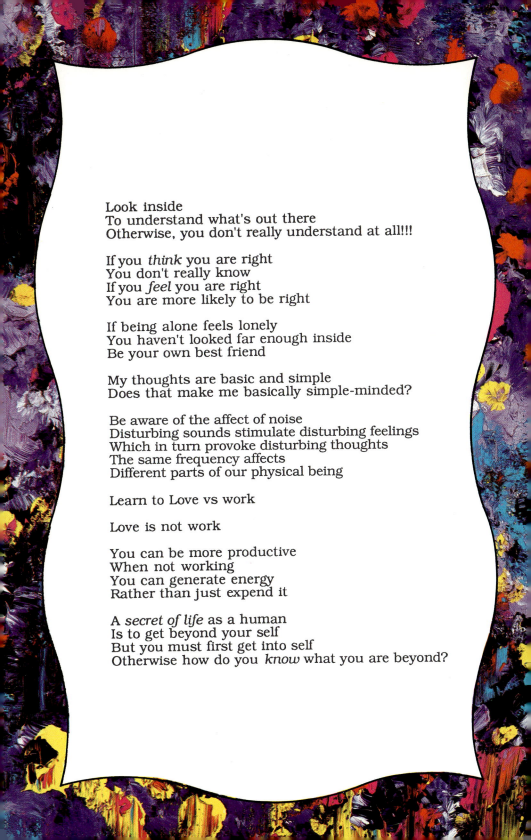

Look inside
To understand what's out there
Otherwise, you don't really understand at all!!!

If you *think* you are right
You don't really know
If you *feel* you are right
You are more likely to be right

If being alone feels lonely
You haven't looked far enough inside
Be your own best friend

My thoughts are basic and simple
Does that make me basically simple-minded?

Be aware of the affect of noise
Disturbing sounds stimulate disturbing feelings
Which in turn provoke disturbing thoughts
The same frequency affects
Different parts of our physical being

Learn to Love vs work

Love is not work

You can be more productive
When not working
You can generate energy
Rather than just expend it

A *secret of life* as a human
Is to get beyond your self
But you must first get into self
Otherwise how do you *know* what you are beyond?

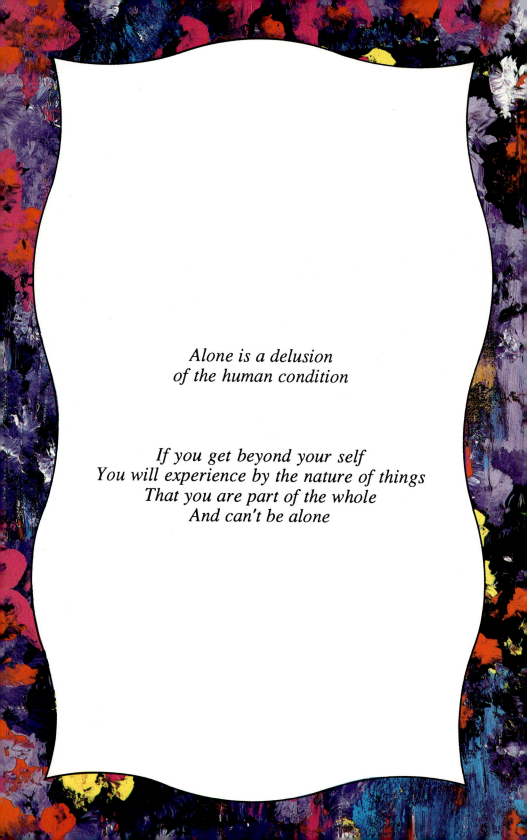

Alone is a delusion
of the human condition

If you get beyond your self
You will experience by the nature of things
That you are part of the whole
And can't be alone

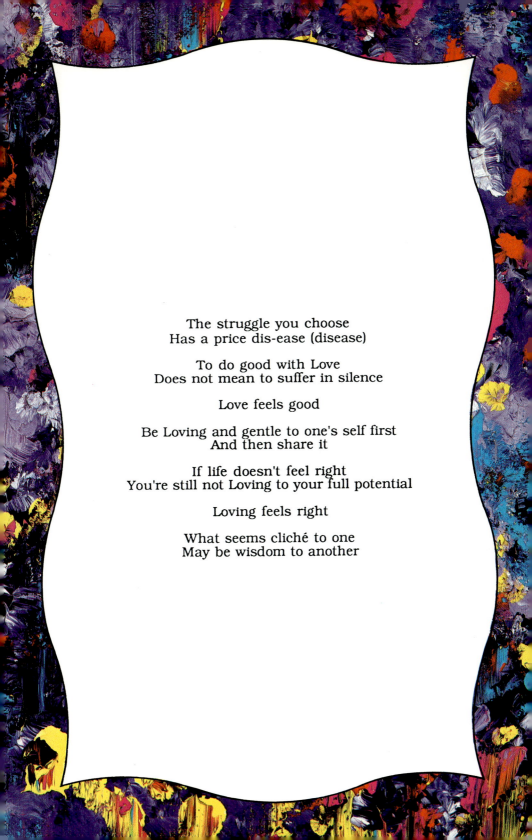

The struggle you choose
Has a price dis-ease (disease)

To do good with Love
Does not mean to suffer in silence

Love feels good

Be Loving and gentle to one's self first
And then share it

If life doesn't feel right
You're still not Loving to your full potential

Loving feels right

What seems cliché to one
May be wisdom to another

Being spiritually aware
And being Spiritual
Are not the same

Many talk good spiritually
But don't live it
The spiritual live it more than talk it

Love, Spirit and Mind
Are all one
Different parts of the same

Love is the feeling
Spirit is the individual identification (rhythm)
Mind is the process of using it

You *don't try* to be spiritual
You choose to be or not to be

Each day get better at it

You don't need to be sick to get better
Just get better and better

Pretending to be spiritual
Is worse than owning up to being a con

You need to be true to where you're at
Or you are nowhere
And going nowhere

Insane   in-sane   sanity
Wouldn't you think insane would be
The epitomé of mental health?

Most seem to sense the Spiritual option
The fact that they can't touch it or eat it
Seems to affect their choice

All you have is the moment
So if you feel you lost something
You're not in the moment!!

There is good and bad in everything

Don't stop with the negatives
Find the flip side
It is your stairway to heaven

If you're not satisfied
Nothing will satisfy you

Awareness is the key to eternal survival
A feeling awareness

You have to work hard
To find out it's not the best way!!!

Once you figure "It" out
"It" works for you

Schools teach you what to think
Not how to think

Need a sense of self
To have you own unique thoughts
Otherwise all you do is
Repeat what you've heard

What most find to be cliché
Is lost wisdom

Distilled Wisdom is knowledge!!!

Most have knowledge
But no Wisdom

Wisdom is what you have
When you experience knowledge
When you learn to live knowledge
You are wise

Being in control is an illusion

Thinking you are in control is a delusion

It's not what happens
It's what you do with it

In and by itself each situation has no meaning
You give it meaning

You may have all the material stuff
But if you don't have Love within you
You really have nothing at all
Somehow all that stuff doesn't hit the ultimate spot

Love is not physical
But it does affect the physical

Life lived is only done with Love
Otherwise it's no more than slow death

Love is energizing and revitalizing
Anything less than Love
Is some level of dis-ease (Stressful)

Reason for being human
Is to learn to be humane
Must find the human spirit

Pure love is the only way
To be one with the whole picture

Pure Love is sharing the *abundance*

Pure Love can only be shared
Once you have Loved your self purely

Learn to live the rhythm

Trying gets you almost there

Take the intensity of love you think
You have for another
Then learn to feel that way for your self
And then share it

Until you feel your own internal Love spot
All other's attempts
Will be futile and addictive

Give to your self first
Then what you feel you need from another
Will be what you want from another
You are the only one who can really
Satisfy your needs

Ultimately no one can do anything to you
Unless you let them

Love gives humans Spirit

Humans talk to humans
Spirits talk to Spirits

Flexibility is the ultimate
In living creatively
Making the most of the moment

You are fine the way you are
You are what you are
Make peace with it
Keep re-fining
Learn from each moment
How to Love more

Life is an ongoing process
Most get so lost in the specifics
They forget where in the process they are

Better learn to enjoy the process
(Reaching your goal)
It's the biggest part of life

The one who enjoys the process
Is more likely to enjoy reaching the goal

The one who crabs through the process
Is a crab

Enjoying the moment
Pretty much ensures one will enjoy the next
Then you are a joy

For a negative person to think positive
Causes discomfort
They are not on the same rhythm

For a positive person to think negative
Causes discomfort

The words you use create your reality
It pays to be a positive thinker

Eliminating negative words
Helps eliminate negative experiences

Ego is limiting
Spirit is expanding

If you have a hard time expressing your self
You are not clear within your self

Insecurities color what you hear and say

Use colors to help balance moods
If a color feels good
Surround your self with it mentally and physically

Saying "I Love you"
Is like talking music
Share the rhythm
It feels better

If you wait for something good to happen
So that you can feel good
You could have a "hell" of a long wait

Feel good and good things happen
They have the same vibration

When a person makes a positive statement
To a negative person
Negative will somehow be heard

See a feel!

Feel a see!!!

I bet the sea
Was first a "wide open see"

Are you one with your surroundings
While aware of your separate uniqueness

Sometimes the most Loving thing
Doesn't look Loving

If someone is being negative
The most positive thing to do
Generate positive to neutralize the negativity

Learn to ask the right question
Therein lies the right answer

To just think is a separatist perspective
To feel you must blend

Get an idea
If you truly believe
It shall be

Life without Love leaves one feeling empty
Look at the many ways people try to fill themselves
With an abundance of "stuff"

Healthy feelings are grounded on healthy emotions
Not on good looks

Feelings are more complex than appearances
Love is a feeling

There is good Love
There is sick love
So if dis-ease is necessary for you
To either give or receive love
It's not the healthy one

How about being Lovingly pampered
(Like when you are sick)
Only do it when healthy

Good Love you share when feeling good

Sick love you get only when you are sick

A union of Spirits coming together
Come-union is communion

Good sex is good sex
Love is Love
Put a heart on!!!

Take sexual energy
Raise it to Mind level (Love)
It increases creativity

Life is nothing more than the
Use or mis-use of your energy

Mind is the Spirit of the Brain

Mind is cosmic
Brain is matcrial

Mind can take you from material to cosmic

If you get stuck in the material
You are missing the best of all
So if you can enjoy the physical, wonderful!
Also, give some time to get the rest!!!

Reality is better than a dream
Love is the only way to know the experience

If you are one with it all
You have the power of it all

Declare it
Then Live it

Get beyond time
And into Love

Wouldn't it be wonderful if all were
Into *Moral* Grandeur?

To get past being a robot
Acknowledge your self

Learn to be free of the limitation
Of the physical senses

Friends have a shared reality

To truly listen
You must get beyond your ego

"To be" takes awhile
You've been trained not "to be"

You were taught what to think
Now do it creatively

How about mutual independence

An experience can amount to nothing
It's what you do with it that counts

The gift in "being" is that it feels good
It's fulfilling; and it's satisfying

Most profess to what they wish they were
Rather than who they are

Body is to soul
What training wheels are to a bike
They help you learn balance

Your physical symptoms
Are *symbols* to learn to adjust to a
Larger scheme of things
When not in the right rhythm there is dis-ease

Feeling good just to feel good
Is worthless

Share a good feeling
Deal with a bad one

We expect from others
That which we don't do for ourselves

Love has no expectations

Feeling Love
Is the up-front reward
Immediate gratification

Without self satisfaction
There is no satisfaction at all

To the person who works hard
Most is hard work

To fine tune your self
Is an ongoing re-finement

Class is classical

We all have soul
Some souls are nicer than others
Spirit makes the difference

Make peace with your soul
Then you can have Spirit

You can't have Love without peace

Love is Love
Sex is sex
To combine the two is wonderful!!!

Life is what you make it
As long as you blame others for what it is
You are helpless and stuck

If you allow someone to be rude to you
Chances are you will somehow be rude to others

What goes around comes around!!

To have thoughts is nice
To be your thoughts even nicer!!!

Take a good thought
And live it for a day

Let the power of the universe blend with you
Don't try to be the power

Love for the wrong reasons breeds contempt
Love for Love breeds Love

Most try to fill time
Learn to use it wisely

Each moment you dwell on what you don't have
Is a moment you miss what is

Be appreciative of what you do have
And make a Loving plan how to
Acquire what you want

Why do most people behave differently
When others are around
Than when alone?

Wouldn't you think people would want
To be the same enthusiastic self
Whether around others or not?

To be or not to be: or what to be
Or how to find out how "to be"!!!

Internal human combustion
        is another force
It's a healing force
It's counter to gravity

When one learns to adjust one's frequency
To the proper vibration (Love)
There's a connection with the power
Of the universes

The power of the universes
Within the human body
Is internal human combustion

Most conversations are really
Nothing more than mutual monologues

If you project that you are better than you feel
You feel inferior
The better part is the real you!

Life can be death
Death can be life
It's all relative!!!

When you share Love with a user
You feel drained
When you share Love with one who has Love
    and respects it
You feel energized
Be aware of the difference

To reduce stress
Admitting to the vulnerabilities
Is half-way out

When you get a thought
If it's right
It will be

Trying gets you almost there

What *seemed* to work for you in the past
May not be effective now
Frustration is an indicator
Time to break an old habit
Replace the old reaction
With a new response

Upset with others
Not living up to your *expectations*
Maybe you aren't living up to your own

Do what you do with meaning for all
Not recognition for one

Many people who look positive are phoney
Exaggerating the good and
Not dealing with the yuck!!!

Ego is self serving
With little regard for others

Spirit is self serving
With the same regard for others

When confident you do for the benefit of others
Not for the approval of others

Feeling good, just to feel good
Is worthless
Sharing a good feeling
Is worth *more*

Deal with a bad feeling
Look it square in the eye
And figure out how to deal with it
Don't be it
Just have it and change it!!!

Even if something feels better
Doesn't mean it feels good

Get a sense of how you want to feel
And go for it
Do all the things in your life that you can
To make it real...and it will be!!!

So if your life is miserable
You made miserable choices
Learn to make better ones
And you will feel better and better...

You may only have miserable choices
At least make the best of what it is
You will feel a bit better
And that at least starts the
Ball rolling in the right direction

What you put into something
Is what you get out of it
So is something for nothing worth nothing?

A death experience
Is a state of Mind
Not a state of brain

It's beyond programming
It's an experience
One *tries* to put into words

Without Love
You have a human animal

With Love
You have a human Spirit

Talk to *your self*
Like you would to a best friend

Be your own best friend
Once you know how it feels
Then you can be one to another

Say to your self
What you wish others would say to you

Appreciate your self

Then when others appreciate
And Love you as much as you Love you
You have real friends
You are on the same rhythm

If you treat your self poorly
Others will treat you similarly

Knowing how something feels
And judging
Are two different things

Knowing the feeling is an experience
Judging is a thought outside your self

In *my* book
Judging is a waste of energy

Be aware of judgements
And replace them with feelings

Feeling out of the Loving rhythm?
Bet you're not having Loving thoughts!!!

We think things to our selves
Things we would never say to another

If you feel rotten

STOP

Take three deep breaths, slowly
(Like a sigh of relief)
Inhale white lite and exhale the tension
Then hear what you were just thinking
(saying to your self)
Replace it with it's Loving counter-part

Loving feelings follow

Smile!!!
It's an automatic enhancer!

You are not just your feelings
Enhance the good
Learn from the bad

Everything is relative
In and by itself
Everything has no meaning
You give it meaning

For Your Thoughts

Love is contagious
Let's start an epidemic

Make the world a better place
Generate good energy
By doing what you do with Love
Others will benefit

If stress is what usually stimulates you
You're not Loving

Love is easy

With Love
    the easier the better!!!

If you still need to prove your self
Thru suffering
You can suffer
Or you can choose the easy option!!!

How you deal with your life
Is all in your choice

When you are ego
You stand alone

When with your Spirit
You are one with it all
And then you have the power of it all

When you are in the moment
There is no time!!

When you are trying to figure out what to do
You don't have all the pieces
Or you would know what to do
Keep looking for more clues
And asking more questions

There is a positive and negative in everything

Negative thoughts are just as valid
As positive thoughts

Positive ones feel good
Negative ones don't

Negative ones are destructive
Positive ones are healing

Your choice to be happy
Depends upon centering on the positives and
Dealing with the negatives

Your individual negatives
Turned to positives with Love
Form your stairway to heaven

We seem to be given the negatives as
Part of the human condition
Why not use them to find the flip-side?
And turn them into your stepping stones to heaven
Instead of boulders weighing you down

Only real purpose in each day
Is to be Loving each moment
And radiate it!!!

Radiate or radiation gets you

If all would radiate Love
The vibration of the planet
Would be much healthier

If someone is hostile
They don't need to say anything
You can feel the vibes
Same with the good ones
   Spread good vibes!!!

If you go through each day crabby
No matter how much you accomplish
You polluted the planet

Stay in good rhythm
Bad things are on a bad rhythm

If you buzz through these elixirs
You aren't going to get the benefit
The experience that comes with contemplation

Rather we all be together
In the rhythm of Love
Than on the frequency of discord

Each frequency has it's own reality!!!

Beauty is in the eye of the beholder
Love is in the Spirit of the feeler

Must deal with negative (outdated) emotions
In order to have valid feelings

Appropriate feelings are more important
Than looks and words

Feeling without understanding
Is a fleeting sensation

With understanding
You know how to keep a Loving feeling
Or at least how to get it back!

Analyzing is separating
Understanding is being one with

If someone means to do well
But never does well
Realize it for what it is
Frustration
Love is missing!

To give feels separate
To share is one with

Image is object of that imagined!!!

Limited options
Lead to addictions

Judging the small picture
Uses a small brain

Experiencing the reality of the cosmos
Takes a *mind*

Just because you are personally involved
You don't need to take it personally

If you take it personally
You loose sight of the bigger picture

Truths are truths
Each lives them differently

There is only one right way
It's called *"with Love"*
But Love has many faces

They say history repeats itself
No, people do

A compulsion to keep doing one thing
Is an addiction

A compulsion to keep doing many things with Love
Is productivity and Heavenly

Every behavior has a consequence

If you feel good
Good things are more likely to happen

What you give off, you get back

To work is not necessarily to be productive
Is the energy you expend somehow benefitting all?

For those who are used to much pain
Feeling extremely good will not seem comfortable
Must learn to enjoy feeling good
Commit to being done with the pain

When you give up your ego
For the bigger picture
It is first you life!!!

When you let go of your ego
You get your Spirit

By giving it up (Ego)
You find that you have it all
But never did!!!
The only thing given up
Is the illusion

Saying affirmations gets you nowhere
Feeling them is to be them

Realize when you're feeling frustrated
It's an indicator that there's an easier way
If you're frustrated, you're not Loving
Vent the tension (i.e. hit a pillow with a tennis racket)
Then find a way to eliminate the
Cause of the frustration

If you're on a better rhythm
You get better answers

When you are feeling afraid
You have abandoned your self

Be your own support system

If you just think
You are separate
To feel is to be one with

If you want to feel good
It just doesn't happen
You need to do things
To make it happen!!!

If you have to justify what you're doing...

...It's bullshit!

If you are on a good rhythm
You get good thoughts

If you are in the present
You are the gift!!!

Once you have the Loving rhythm
The test is to keep it
Thru learning how to
Incorporate each day's new lessons

You never give anything up
You just acquire better choices

What looks right in the 3rd dimension
Doesn't usually feel right in the 4th

When you do for the bigger picture's benefit
Then it's Pure Truth (LOVE)

Have you acquired "it all" by societies standards?
But still feel there's something missing?
It's Love
As long as ego controls something *is* missing

If all around you is abrasive
You vibrate at a similar frequency

Everything has a vibration
"To be" is your natural vibe

Why not do something to impress your self
Be wonderful to you!!!

Awareness of self
Helps you deal effectively
Otherwise life deals with you

Just because you accept things the way they are
Doesn't mean you have to like it or be around it

For most, if they wouldn't have to do anything
They would have nothing to do
Or they would do nothing at all

Love is a motivator

Your Spirit is your true energizer
But you must be true to it first

Most use the physical as
An end unto itself
It's just a tool
To get another beginning

You won't find your human Spirit
Looking in the mirror

Every rhythm has a different reality

Love is ...so you can't make Love
But you can share it!!!

If you do with Love
It works; not you

If you are needy
You will find the needy

If you are Loving
You will find the Loving

Do from the abundance of Love
Not from need

Build on what is
Instead of pretending what isn't

Go from what you *thought* it should be
To how you *feel* it is
And make the most of it

Each moment is a gift
Appreciate it as such

The more you feel good
The more good you do

Spirit is electric
Body is magnetic
(You are an electro-magnet)

As long as you make things happen your way
You limit your self

Inklings help us reach our potential
Follow the inklings

Peace is an internal state
Which is reflected outwardly

You don't have it
You must be one with it

Humans are creatures of habit
Habit limits awareness to opportunities

To give up one's self for the bigger picture
Doesn't mean to surrender who you are
It means to be the best you can
For your self as well as the betterment of all

Giving one's self up
Means to be part of it all
Instead of walking around as
Separate and struggling thru it

By giving it up
You find out you have it all
But never did

The last person most listen to
Is their self. (Start really listening)

What makes you feel good about you and your life?
Aside from $ and $ related stuff

Most get caught up in the everyday issues!
Better to see them as symbols
To a greater scheme of things

Learn to refine your rhythm (vibration)
Thru the use of unsettling symbols

Learn to exchange negative symbols
To enhancing experiences

All have soul
But without Spirit
You have a lost soul

Love and Spirit are on the same rhythm

Your soul can identify with the negative
If you let it!!
The choice is yours
Be with the Loving and you have Spirit
Be with the negative and you have "hell"

Once you have learned the Loving lesson
The pain goes away

Your problems aren't an end unto themselves
Problems dealt with Love
Are you stairway to heaven

Either you deal with the issues
Or the issues deal with you

Life is an experience
Not a view or a taste or a touch

Magnify the positive!!!

When you acquire a bigger view
The issue is relatively smaller

To get past an issue
You must learn the lesson
Then forgiveness
Isn't an issue

To forgive another
You must first make peace with your self

Only way to forgive is
Thru increased awareness
What is there to be learned
From the particular situation

Learn to be more Loving
Because of it (whatever *it* is)

If you blame another
You are not taking complete responsibility
You will be dependent and somewhat helpless

At least be in control of being out of control

Change "have to's" to "want to's"

If you "have to" I'm sure
You don't "want to"

Aging is due to resistance

We bring things upon our selves
To learn the Loving lesson
Which then takes one to a more
Refined frequency of Love

Heaven and Love are on the same frequency!!!

We all get the right thoughts
Better if you learn to be them

We all have thoughts
It's what you do with them that counts

Take a thought
Give it meaning
Use it in your life!

To truly listen
You must get past your ego (personality)

Unabandoned exhilaration is what you get
When you get beyond what the physical senses crave

Most have *abandoned* exhilaration
Always making up for something lost
Their Loving Spirit

As one re-fines one's self
The finer one's tastes

Every right answer is on the right rhythm
It's called Love

If you are in to it
You intuit

Nothing stays the same
Why do people keep treating it so?

All is vibration
Learn to sense the rhythm of it

Until you are morally fit
Your Spirit is not with your soul (self)

See what you would like to be like
In order to be more morally fit
Then step inside that picture
And be it!!!

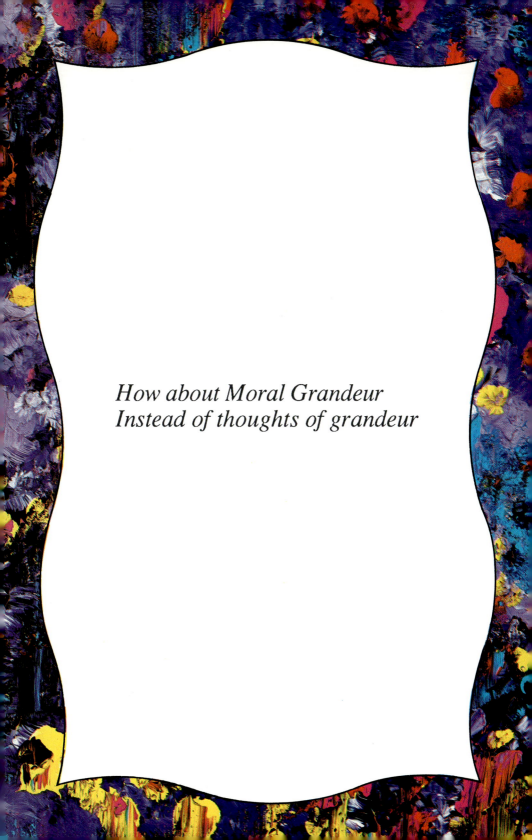

How about Moral Grandeur
Instead of thoughts of grandeur

Realize when you are frustrated
Figure out the cause
Learn the Loving lesson

Find a way to *vent* the *tension*
(Hit a pillow with a tennis racket, scream etc.)
You will feel more relaxed and on another frequency
Now on a mellower rhythm: you will find mellow
Solutions

If you are working hard
At staying in control or getting control
You are fighting the flow

Your body is your tool
The intensity of pain it exudes
Is relative to how
Far off your natural rhythm (vibration)

The manifester of the form
Got lost in the form
And forgot what manifested it

When you are in each moment with Love
You come out wise
Not victimized

Wisdom and Love
Are on the same wavelength

Love is *feeling* to the Nth degree

All is vibration
Connect with the greatest vibration of all
Pure Love

You have a natural frequency (rhythm)
Learn to settle in "with it"
Then you can first enhance it

Color, music and fragrances
All have diverse vibrations

Use color, music and fragrance
To help you get to and stay
With your natural rhythm

You will know which to blend with
They will enhance your sense of
"Being" one with "It all"

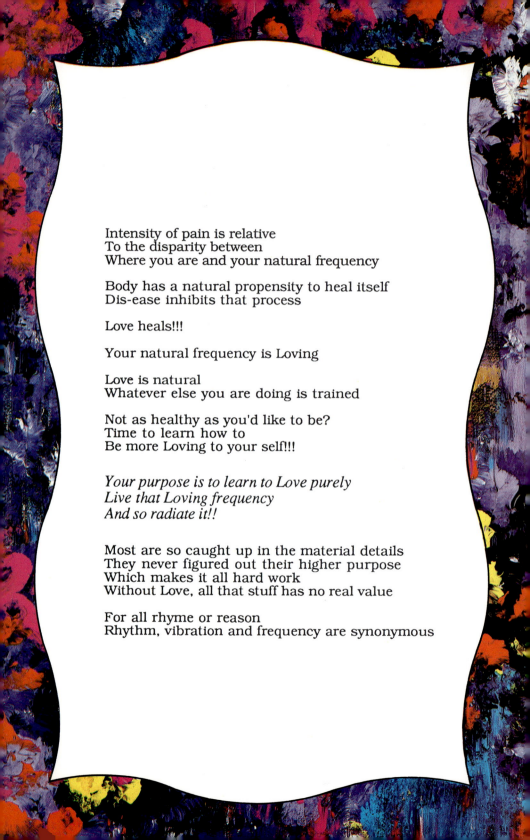

Intensity of pain is relative
To the disparity between
Where you are and your natural frequency

Body has a natural propensity to heal itself
Dis-ease inhibits that process

Love heals!!!

Your natural frequency is Loving

Love is natural
Whatever else you are doing is trained

Not as healthy as you'd like to be?
Time to learn how to
Be more Loving to your self!!!

Your purpose is to learn to Love purely
Live that Loving frequency
And so radiate it!!

Most are so caught up in the material details
They never figured out their higher purpose
Which makes it all hard work
Without Love, all that stuff has no real value

For all rhyme or reason
Rhythm, vibration and frequency are synonymous

Do it (whatever you're doing) with Love
Or it's "bull shit"

If you are not with the bigger picture
You will feel lazy!!
You feel enthusiastic when you do with Love

For all the work you've done
What have you really accomplished?

After a certain point
It doesn't matter why
Just figure out how to
Make the most of what is with Love

You can't really make it what *you* want
And get the best!

To get the best!!
Make the most of what is!!!
First you gotta know "what is"

It's not what's out there
It's what's in there!!!!!!!

Out there is only reflective
Of what's in there

Feelings give words power!!!

Most are never quite honest with their emotions
And consequently, their intentions!!

It's not so much what you do
But how you do it
It's all in the *attitude*

There is no such thing as a handicap
There is just another way!

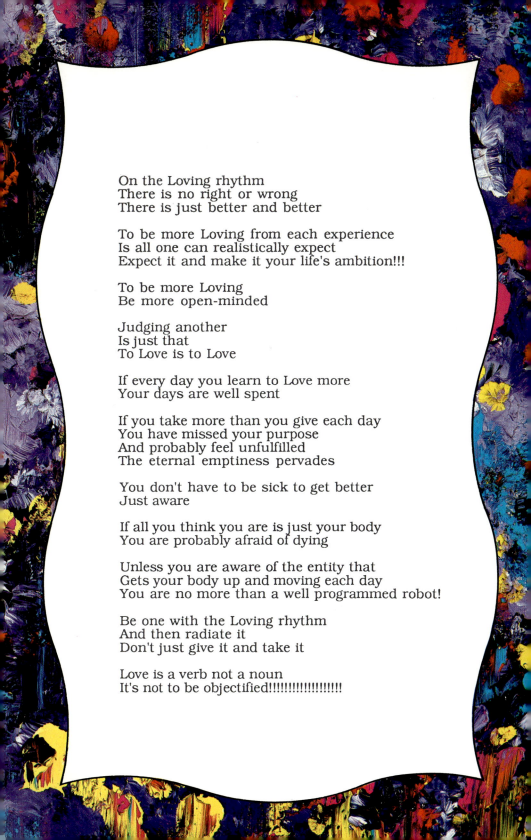

On the Loving rhythm
There is no right or wrong
There is just better and better

To be more Loving from each experience
Is all one can realistically expect
Expect it and make it your life's ambition!!!

To be more Loving
Be more open-minded

Judging another
Is just that
To Love is to Love

If every day you learn to Love more
Your days are well spent

If you take more than you give each day
You have missed your purpose
And probably feel unfulfilled
The eternal emptiness pervades

You don't have to be sick to get better
Just aware

If all you think you are is just your body
You are probably afraid of dying

Unless you are aware of the entity that
Gets your body up and moving each day
You are no more than a well programmed robot!

Be one with the Loving rhythm
And then radiate it
Don't just give it and take it

Love is a verb not a noun
It's not to be objectified!!!!!!!!!!!!!!!!!!!

For the perfectionist
The most you can be is
Perfect at not being perfect

The only thing that will save you
On a polluted planet
Is to be on a pure rhythm
If on a polluted frequency
You will be one with the mess

Get in touch with your essence
Essence is the feeling of oneness
Beyond form

Love is not physical
As heaven is not earth

First learn to use your body as a tool
Learn the meaning behind your physical symptoms
Then you can get beyond the purely physical

Rhythm is real
Relatively speaking
Physical is no-thing

When someone tells you to be patient
Know where patience ends and ignorance begins

You have to get into matter
To realize it doesn't matter

If you have a sense of self
There is no judging
If you don't have a sense of self
That's all there is (judging)

Honesty is relative to neediness

If you want love real bad
You get bad love

Words,
In and by themselves have no meaning
Your experiences
Give them meaning

So, it's not so much what you say
(the words you use)
It's more the attitude
With which you say them

What you do in one part of your life
Affects all parts of your life
It's all part of the bigger picture

Most take the beaten path
And so get beat
They're on the same rhythm
Find your own unique path

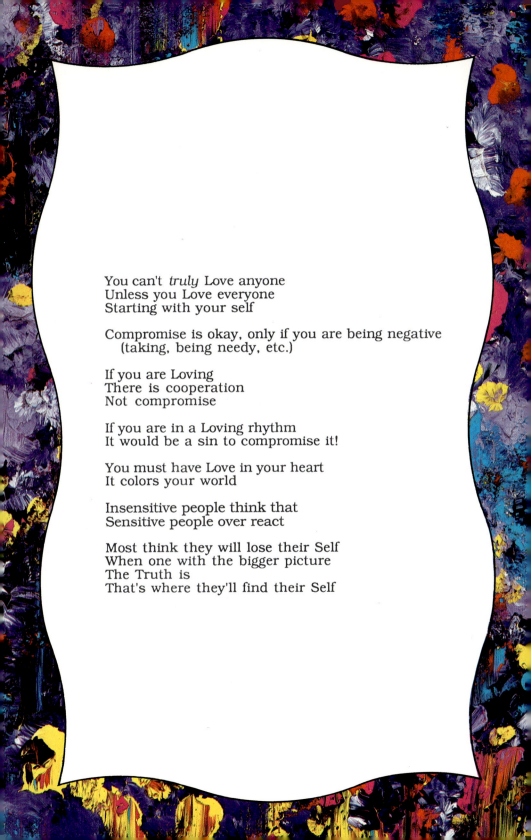

You can't *truly* Love anyone
Unless you Love everyone
Starting with your self

Compromise is okay, only if you are being negative
   (taking, being needy, etc.)

If you are Loving
There is cooperation
Not compromise

If you are in a Loving rhythm
It would be a sin to compromise it!

You must have Love in your heart
It colors your world

Insensitive people think that
Sensitive people over react

Most think they will lose their Self
When one with the bigger picture
The Truth is
That's where they'll find their Self

When you are in the rhythm of Love
Time doesn't fly
You do!!!

In the rhythm of Love
There is no time

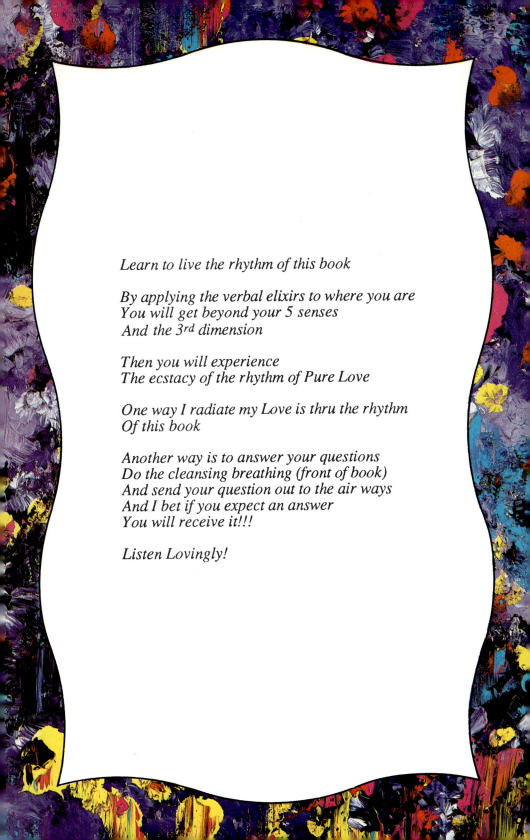

Learn to live the rhythm of this book

By applying the verbal elixirs to where you are
You will get beyond your 5 senses
And the 3rd dimension

Then you will experience
The ecstacy of the rhythm of Pure Love

One way I radiate my Love is thru the rhythm
Of this book

Another way is to answer your questions
Do the cleansing breathing (front of book)
And send your question out to the air ways
And I bet if you expect an answer
You will receive it!!!

Listen Lovingly!

For Your Thoughts

For Your Thoughts

For Your Thoughts